neon

/ˈniːɒn/

noun

noun: **neon**; symbol: **Ne**

1. the chemical element of atomic number 10, an inert gaseous element of the noble gas group. It is obtained by the distillation of liquid air and is used in fluorescent lamps and illuminated advertising signs.
2. fluorescent lighting or signs using neon or another gas.
"the lobby of the hotel was bright with neon"

- a small lamp containing neon.

plural noun: **neons**
"neons indicate the state of the mains wiring"

- very bright or fluorescent in colour.

modifier noun: **neon**
"she had recently dyed her hair neon pink"

Origin

late 19th century: from Greek, literally 'something new', neuter of the adjective *neos* .

Spark
You M

ETERNI

JOIN
CIPATE
SHARE
CH
LEBRATE
RT

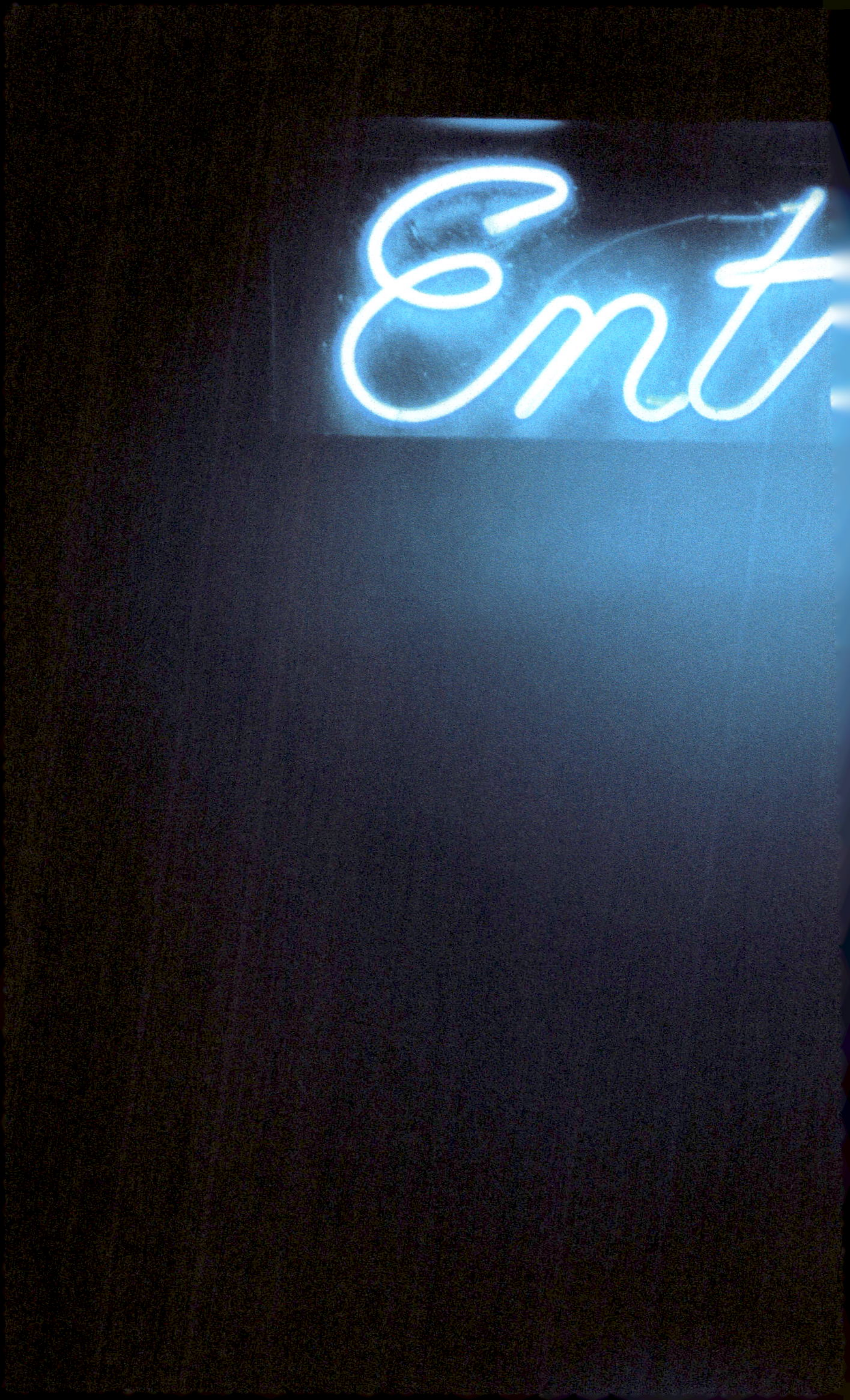
Ent

ance

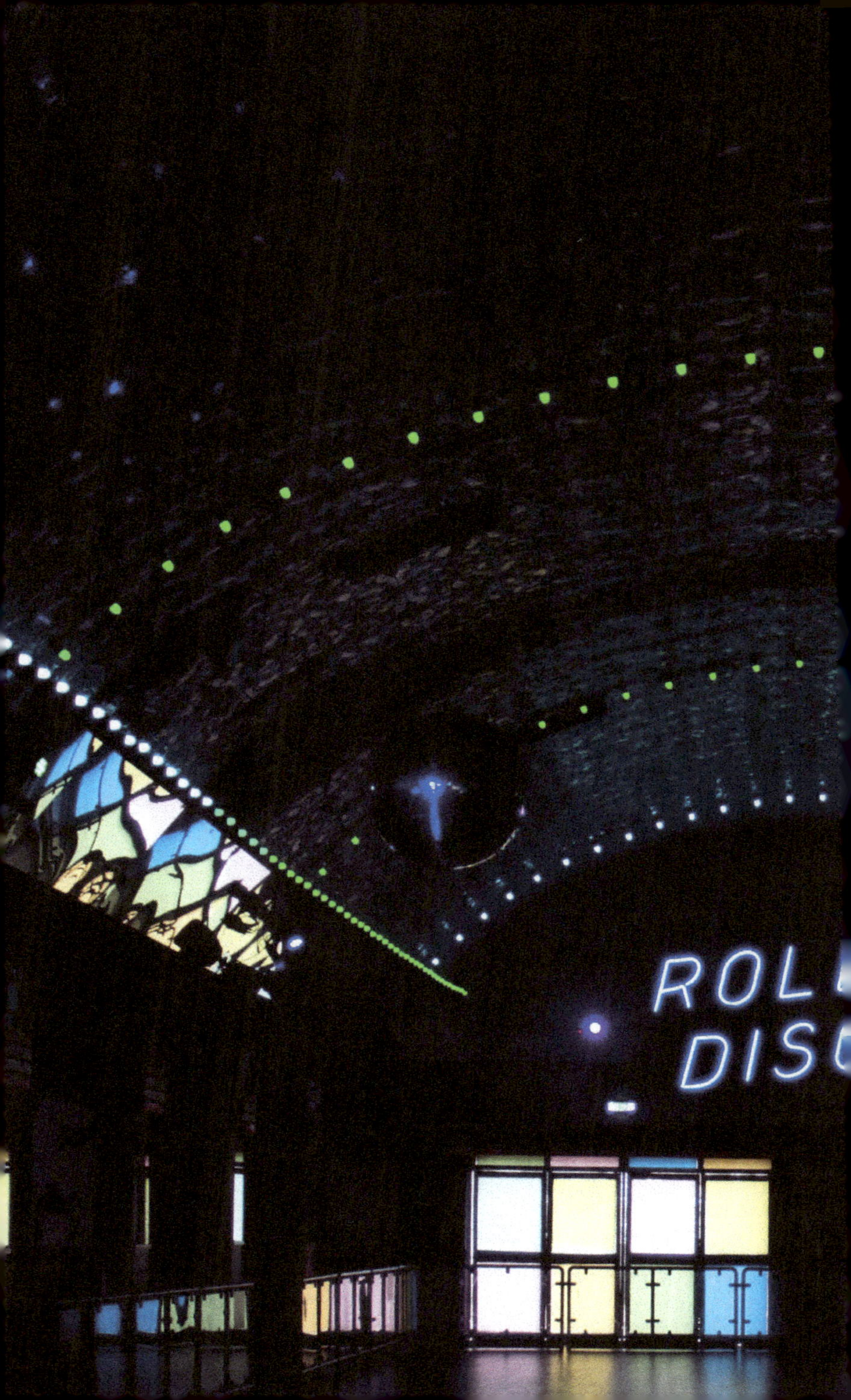
ROL
DISC

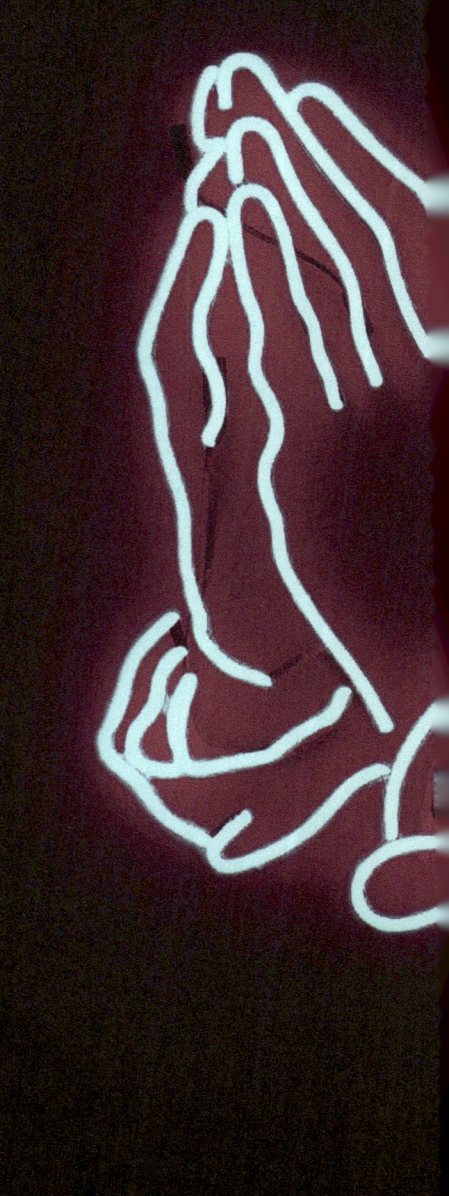

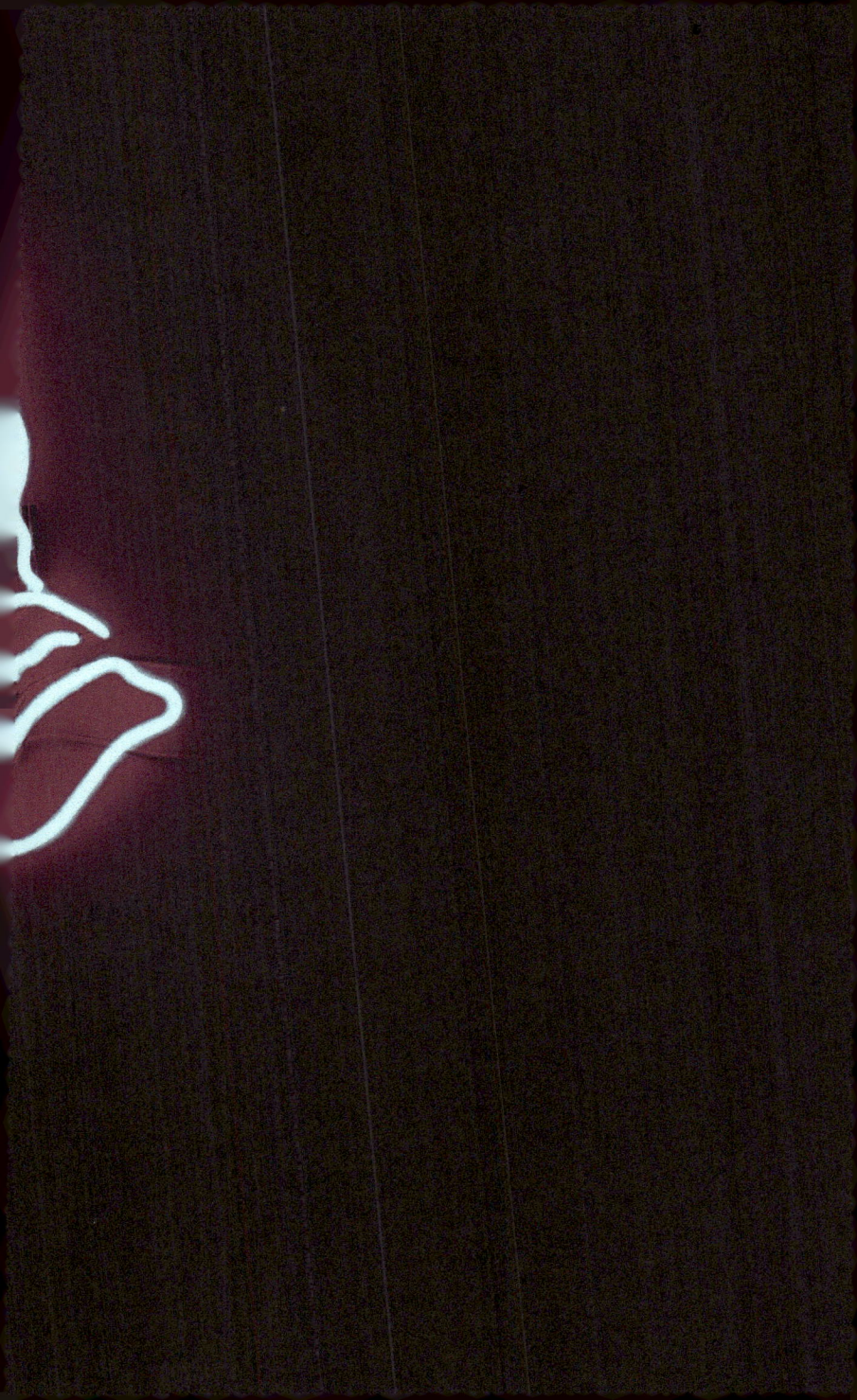

ING GREAT

LOVE

LOVE is A RIGHT

LOVE is LOVE

live and let love

Support LOVE

LOVE wins

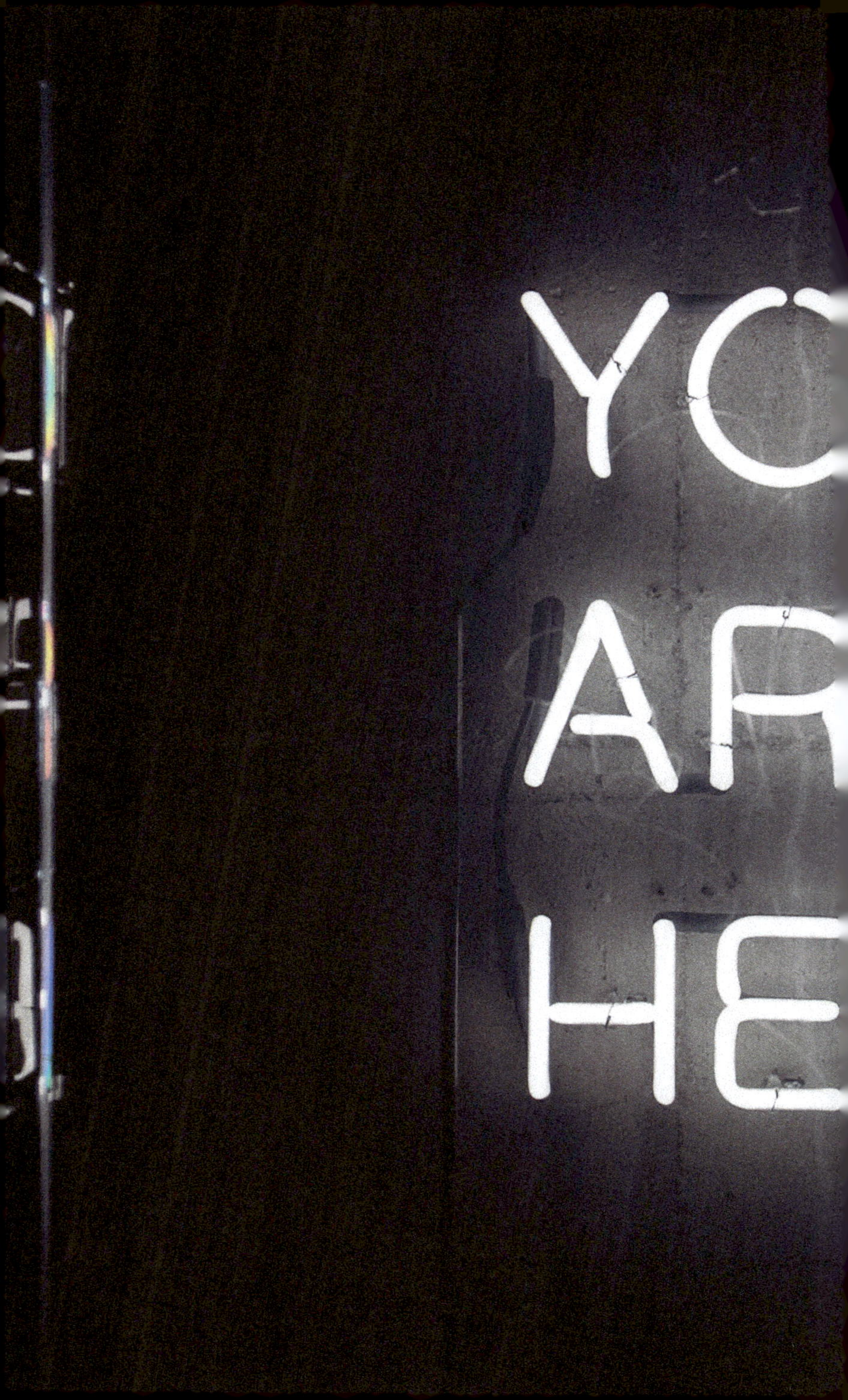
YO
AR
HE

WORK HARD

Be th

You w

In the

Buzz

to See

World

CPSIA information can be obtained
at www.ICGtesting.com
Printed in the USA
BVHW060937220419
546161BV00015B/486/P

9 780368 592737